THREE FRIENDS IN A BOAT

The *Carn Ingli*

THREE FRIENDS IN A BOAT

Memoir of a cruise to the Mediterranean

Patrick Inglis Melia

Three Friends in a Boat

is published in 2011 by
ARLEN HOUSE
an imprint of Arlen Publications Ltd
42 Grange Abbey Road
Baldoyle
Dublin 13
Ireland
Phone/Fax: 353 86 8207617
Email: arlenhouse@gmail.com

Distributed internationally by
SYRACUSE UNIVERSITY PRESS
621 Skytop Road, Suite 110
Syracuse, NY 13244–5290
Phone: 315–443–5534/Fax: 315–443–5545
Email: supress@syr.edu

ISBN 978–1–85132–019–6, paperback
ISBN 978–1–85132–021–9, hardback

Typesetting ¦ Arlen House
Printing ¦ Brunswick Press
Cover Image ¦ Melia family collection

Contents

Acknowledgements

The author and publisher wish to thank:

Pauline Bewick
Conor and Eileen Kavanagh
Adrienne Foran and Brunswick Press
Poppy Melia
Aran Mulvihill
Conor Mulvihill
Adam Mulvihill
Holly Melia
Denise Cook Melia
Nina Finn-Kelcey
Maria Simonds-Gooding
Regine Bartsch and Mike O'Neill
Fiona Carr
Countess Heidi Von Wedel
Fiona MacCormack
Kate Landers
Madeleine Crowley
Edso Crowley
The late Michael Ahern
Tom Frank O'Connor
Ed Cowan and Nuala Fitzgerald Cowan

for Pauline

Three Friends in a Boat

Pat Melia

Barry Laverty

Philip Castle

Map of the Journey fron Chicester Harbour to Valletta

Drawn by Aran Mulvihill

Chapter I

ENGLAND

The three friends were Philip, Barry and Pat. The boat was the *Carn Ingli*, a converted RNLI sea-going boat, length forty-two feet, double diagonal mahogany hull, Perkins diesel, ketch rigged. A motor sailor; couldn't be safer, you say, and you would have been right. Our destination was Malta, a stepping stone in the Mediterranean. We planned a departure from Chichester Harbour and the boat was moored in the last pound of the Chichester Canal. Philip and Barry had sailed her down from the north-east coast developing a taste for the white fish from those cool waters and consuming them, even for breakfast. Barry, despite her name, was female, and she and Philip were engaged.

Pat Melia on the Carn Ingli, *1960*

I joined them in Dover. We sailed on the ebbing tide which swept us down channel effortlessly past the low shingle beach of Dungeness to the mighty headlands and white-chalk cliffs that fronted the South Downs. After Seaford Head, its beach contained by orderly groins, we passed up the little river at Newhaven, making a tentative approach between the rows of wooden piers on either side of the river. Philip, our skipper, at the helm.

'Good afternoon Mr. Castle, welcome to New Haven. We can offer you mooring on Pier 47'.

A young uniformed man grinned from the Harbour Master's Office on an admirable PA system. How did he know Philip's name? Simple – an annual publication identifying all registered yachts in Britain. Well it's a maritime nation. Admiralty charts are similarly impressive. Philip and Barry spent the night and many nights to come on the Chichester Canal mooring, where we fitted out the *Carn Ingli*. I caught the little stopping-train back to my job in London and came down at weekends to help with the work.

Like most such projects this took an inordinately, continuously multiplying, length of time. At first I was to-ing and fro-ing, starting on my little Peugeot motorbike shortly after sunrise; up to the beech wood behind the town, occasionally glimpsing a deer in the dim light under the trees above Goodwood Race Course. On and down to suburbia, shiny cars, to the psychiatric hospital where I worked. But quite soon the boat became my home. I finished my London job and went to live full-time on it. Philip, Barry and I were the crew and this became our world. My berth was in the fore-peak, quite comfortable, a bit bouncy when driving into a choppy sea, but dry, unless I forgot to close the sea cock.

It was the early summer of 1960, warm and sunny and we set to with paint remover, scrapers, varnish and paint (white with light-green trim). Philip dispatched me to the Chandlers in Chichester to get a book on astral navigation; I thought: 'he really means business'. Unfortunately he was disappointed in my purchase, it was too elementary for him. Eventually he got a splendid textbook on the subject, though we continued the simplest dead reckoning whenever we strayed from easily recognised sea and land marks.

But there was much to do before we could even lock out of the Chichester Canal. Next came rigging and stepping the masts. We managed these ourselves; the feet of the masts were hinged and could be winched to raise the mast to the vertical. Then the shrouds had to support the masts. Their tension could be adjusted by bottle screws, but alas at this stage they had seized up. Tommy bars, penetrating oil and blow lamps were deployed and after some days of frustrated endeavour, the screws gave up their seemingly invincible grip and surrendered to our persistence – which it must be said was almost entirely due to Philip's good work.

The Carn Ingli

Now it was time to fine tune the rigging to see that the masts were nicely aligned and correctly raked. This task required much skill and fine judgment and Philip gave the job to two professionals; and professionals they were of the ultimate prestige: two former Royal Navy seamen. They were brisk and highly competent. They busied themselves about the boat, tightening this and slackening that, occasionally instructing us. 'That's not a knot, it's an itch'. They quickly tensioned the shrouds, until she was beautifully tuned like a cello, a work of art, and then after good humoured goodbyes they were off.

Chapter II

Crossing the Channel

At last we were ready for the cruise. The first port of call was to be Le Havre and we left the still waters of the Chichester Canal early in the morning, locking out into Chichester Harbour. We cast off and suddenly the tempo of life aboard the *Carn Ingli* changed. It was my job as deck-hand to pull in the heavy mooring warps and springs, our last contact with *terra firma,* and to coil them neatly on deck, then to stow them by the Samson and stern posts. I had looked forward to the *Carn Ingli* slipping downstream and taking in the sights of the harbour, but in the event I was so busy with my unfamiliar tasks that by the time everything was done we were at the harbour mouth. I did manage to see the fleet of racing Flying Fifteens: and a fine sight they made. They are small keel-boats, fast and elegant. Their most illustrious skipper and crew being Prince Philip and Uffa Fox, the latter also their designer.

We passed out of Chichester Harbour between the low sandy hills of Hayling Island and West Wittering and were met by a stiff breeze blowing from Spithead. We pounded against the choppy waves, pitching and throwing off a bow wave of white spray. Barry had retired into the cabin. I was beginning to feel sick. Philip began groaning and asked me to take over the helm. As I did so he slumped down on his side and lay on the wheelhouse deck in his immaculate white long trousers and shirt. That left me to sail the boat. Immediately I felt completely better. Philip did a body count and reported an improvement in his *mal de mer*. Barry kept to the cabin reading books about the sea.

Barry Laverty

The wind increased but the sun shone. Philip broke the news that we had a low ebbing tide and would not be able to re-enter Chichester Harbour until late in the day. Mindful of Cannute we accepted the news with reasonably good spirit. The plan was that we would stand off and on until we could sail back into Chichester Harbour. This we did with commendable patience and for company we had *The Britannia,* the royal yacht, which steamed up the Channel and then turned into the Spithead.

When Philip judged that we had enough water over the Chichester Bar we made for the bay to the north of Hayling Island and there we dropped anchor for the night.

Early next morning the sky was light blue, the sea calm and the sun opalescent. Perfect, you might think, but the radio shipping forecast firmly announced 'Wight; Gale Force 8 …' Philip was unabashed and said that he knew this coast well, that it was an ideal day to cross the Channel and that we would be fools to miss it.

Philip was a physics student and it seemed to me that he had a deep understanding of meteorology and I accepted his judgment, as did Barry. So she and I made our way to the foredeck and winched up the anchor, deeply satisfied by the rattle of its chain.

Philip Castle

'Sic fatur lacremans immitit pro rogas ad pelagos'

None of us had sailed out of sight of land before and so Virgil's words had the appropriate heroic quality as we passed the Nab Tower and turned our prow to the open sea, setting our compass course for the headland a little to the east of Le Havre. By this time the shipping forecast had dropped their Gale Force 8 warning and the weather seemed set fair. For me, one of the charms of off-shore sailing is that nothing much happens for long periods of time, which is conducive to a state of dreamy meditation from which the incidents of the day or night form a stark contrast and may require a rapid and accurate response. In this way it resembles cricket, though in the latter case, of course, it is a cricketer who has to make the response, not a spectator.

I shoved my head out of the port side of the wheel-house and there filling my field of vision was an enormous futuristic airplane. There was a gigantic booming sound, all the noise of the plane travelling near the speed of sound almost catching up with it. The black plane just above the wave tops diminished in size rapidly and streaked like an arrow towards its consort, a grey etheral aircraft carrier about two miles away and at the last moment revealed its wings, and shot vertically to the heavens until it disappeared from sight and that was that. But we did debate whether he was sent to vet us for possible threat to the carrier, or was it a jolly prank played on naive yachtsmen.

Back to the dreamy meditation, but not for long. Something has happened. The faint smudges barely discernable up-channel have changed into a long procession of merchant-men sailing downchannel in line-ahead formation two or three cables distance between each, travelling at about 15 knots, the speed difficult to estimate. A fine sight with their bright paintwork shining in the sunny breeze. But what are we going to do? How are we going to penetrate their tight formation and get on the southern, French side of the line. We discussed it briefly. Our skipper decided that we would cross the wake of one of the ships close to its stern, thus giving us as much time as possible to get out of the way of the following ship. None of us was really sure who had the right of way and certainly none of us wanted to try conclusions with one of the enormous merchant-men. So on we went. We knew that once we had crossed the wake and could see the onward-coming merchant-man's portside, we would be safe. But instead of slipping behind us, the peak of the bow of the following ship followed us and started to bear down on us. It was a frightening few seconds (it felt like minutes). I looked up at the lone helmsman on the bridge of the merchant-man and after a few moments he swung back onto his course and his joke was over. This was one of the many times I have vowed to give up sailing and take up carpet bowls instead.

The Carn Ingli

It is now dark. We are sailing for Cap d'Antifer, a prominent seamark about twenty miles north-east up the coast from Le Havre. Once we close with the coast, we will turn south-west and hug the coast until we get to Le Havre. It is my spell at the wheel. What is required is that I should steer in a straight line for Cap d'Antifer, not so easy in the dark because the lighthouse only flashes once every twenty seconds. To my surprise its flash does not appear dead ahead where I expected it, but maybe as much as 30° or 40° degrees of deviation from our hoped for course. Correction was a struggle, but at last we were hugging the coast, not too close in, and keeping a keen eye out for the pier-head lights leading us into Le Port de Havre. Suddenly I saw lights about twenty feet above us. After a few moments of astonishment, I realised we were about to ram a lead-in light buoy for the port channel. I had never seen a big buoy for ocean-going ships before and didn't recognize what it was immediately, but just in time I put the helm down and we swung to starboard, narrowly missing the enormous structure swaying just above and ahead of us. It was all over very quickly and I don't think Philip and Barry down in the cabin realised how near we were to a collision.

At last we were in the port and we made for some brightly-lit huts where we thought that we might find the office of the Capitaine de Port. Indeed we did and were given peremptory instructions as to where we should moor. I have to admit that any lack of cordiality in our exchanges may have been due to our meagre grasp of the French language, rather than any slight truculence in the part of our gallic hosts. Anyway we made our way back to the outer harbour and dropped our best bower, with a kedge over the stern to stop us from swinging out into the fairway running in towards the moorings for small craft; and so to bed.

Chapter III

The French Canals

At Trinity College, both Philip and I had sat at the feet of the Professor of Physics, Ernest Walton, Nobel Laureate. He began each lecture with the words 'Now, last day we …' and he went on to give the main points of last day's lesson. It would have been better had Philip and I been more attentive. The lesson was, I think, keep away from large merchant ships. We had a busy day ahead of us. We had to find our way through the complex Port du Havre from the little port for small craft with its delightful glimpses of the open sea, through to the busy port and thence into the Canal de Tancarville. This would take us parallel to the out-going River Seine and would enable us to bypass the shoal banks in the Seine Estuary. So onward!

The harbour had become quite narrow and there were ships moored along the quays. This made it necessary for Philip to put the boat astern to make a three-point turn. First, we went ahead cautiously, turning to starboard so that we headed for a cargo vessel moored to the quay. As we approached it and Philip put our engine astern, the engine cut out leaving us to drift rapidly towards the cargo boat with no apparent means of stopping. He folded his arms, accepting the inevitable. Barry and I retreated from the anticipated point of impact nastily under the curve of the stern. Suddenly it dawned on Philip that he might be able to restart our engine, it fired and he put it into reverse. Full speed astern. The water between the two boats churned furiously and our propeller just managed to pull away, and off we went to the Canal de Tancarville. Things were quieter now. To the east were the low hills of Normandy. To the west was a swarm of brightly painted oil tanks, behind them the Seine Estuary. Our canal led away from the turbulent waters of the Channel towards the distant mammoth road bridge which soared through the air on its way to span the canal and estuary. We tied up in the shadow of the mighty Pont de Normandy and strolled to a restaurant tucked away there and enjoyed inordinately our first dinner of the trip.

Barry Laverty

Next morning we walked down to the last lock on the canal to see how locking out was managed; a wise precaution. The tide was flowing, and flowing very fast. The crews of the narrow *péniches* were past masters at this manoeuvre. When ascending the river they pulled out with their bow as far downstream as possible and then motored out quickly until the stream caught the bow and whipped the barge away up-river. Hey presto! But then we had to do the trick, and we did quite credibly. We motored on in great style on the fast up-going tide, enjoying the tautness of our rig so expertly installed by our naval friends at Chichester. But we knew that the enjoyment was to be short-lived – we were to drop down the masts on deck at Rouen so that we could pass under the bridges above that point. The Seine was tidal and its banks were scraggy due to their twice-daily exposure. Mooring was achieved by tying up to the bushes. We came to an area where the banks were flattened out and replaced by quays strewn with heaps of coal. We found a place to moor and de-rig the boat.

Next morning we walked up to the centre of the town and saw the magnificent cathedral built on a slight eminence presiding over the gentle plain of Normandy, immortalized in Monet's stupendous paintings of four stages of its day.

The river now took a slow serpentine course marked by the worn chalk cliffs rising out of the woods. We stopped at Les Andelys, the first, a little village built on the east bank of the river; the second at the end of a straight avenue leaving the river and ending in the village square. We did our shopping and had lunch in a large rather gloomy hotel in the riverine Andelys. I was looking forward to seeing Argenteuil where so many impressionists had painted. It turned out not to be a pretty riverside village, but a rather grubby industrial town. The march of material progress you might think? But no. On a more recent visit to Paris, I went to the Musée d'Orsay and looked at a Monet and lo, in the left-hand corner of it was the tell-tale chimney stack belching smoke, diminished in size, but nevertheless unmistakable, somewhat disillusioning that our beloved impressionists could be guilty of prettifying their pictures. In Paris we tied up at the comfortable boat house of the French Cruising Club lying on the right bank just below La Place de la Concorde.

We had showers, walked up through the *Quartier latin* and had dinner amongst the clatter of students and artists at the superlative Polydor. But even the delights of Paris couldn't detain us from the rivers and canals leading to the Mediterranean. Shortly after leaving the suburbs of the great city, at the confluence of the Seine and the Yonne, we turned south into the Yonne, towards the distant hills through which we must pass to reach the next stage in our journey, Burgundy.

Soon we were in the depths of the country, often far from roads. Barry and I carried our baskets across the fields to little villages where we would buy our provisions. Back on the river, fishermen guarded their rods jealously with menacing threats lest we disturb their chosen spots by passing too close in the boat. We passed from the Yonne through a lock into the Canal de Bourgogne. The day was punctuated by rising through occasional locks. The lock gate would be open as we approached it. As deck hand I would wait in the bows and as we went into the lock I would grab the lock ladder and scramble ashore. Barry would pass the two mooring lines to me, the lock-keeper would close the lock gates and let in water from the higher pounds ahead of us, and when we became level with the higher pound the lock-keeper would open the upper gate. I would collect the mooring lines, jump aboard and on we would go, floating a dozen or two feet higher in the landscape, heading always for the gentle hills of Burgundy.

Navigation began at 6.30am and finished at 6.30pm. This was the published rule. The canals were fairly busy. A common cargo was grain, which was carried in the deep open hold of the *péniche.* The conical hill made by the grain was often surmounted by a vigorous cock who encouraged the hens to supply the human family who lived and worked on the barge. The children played happily and didn't seem to have to go to school.

Barry Laverty

One evening on the close of navigation we were glad to find a row of trees running along the side of the canal, ideal for mooring we thought. A mooring line fore and aft and we went below to the *Carn Ingli's* comfortable saloon where Barry, who loved cooking, was preparing dinner.

'*Carn Ingli,* attention', came an imperious voice.

I climbed up on deck. Standing up on the tow path was a large-sized oldish man. He had no English and I had virtually no French, but to offset this he was a very good if somewhat noisy communicator. He rapidly made it clear that we had obstructed the tow path with our mooring ropes and that this could not be tolerated. After much shouting '*vous ne avez pas la droite*' and gesturing, he gradually cooled down and indicated that he would save the day with a pair of crow bars. He went off and returned shortly with the two bars which he called 'piques'. He drove them into the canal bank, one for the bow rope, the other for the stern, leaving the tow path unobstructed as it should be, and we all beamed at each other with much satisfaction.

We slept soundly and next day resumed our journey through the pretty countryside of north-central France. From this we must cross the hills leading to Burgundy and thence descend into the vast sunny valleys of the Soane and Rhone which lead to the south. Rivers and canals do not cross mountains easily, and in this case it was done by means of a tunnel. The carbon monoxide generated by the engines of the barges, and indeed by the *Carn Ingli*, would be highly toxic in the long narrow tunnel. '*On mouerts dans une demi heur*'. Normally this was dealt with by an electric motor which ran along under the roof of the tunnel and to which the barges attached themselves and could be towed harmlessly the length of the tunnel. But alas the electric motor had broken down. So another strategy was deployed. The barges motored through the tunnel, each under its own power, and after it had negotiated the tunnel and proceeded on its way, the next barge would have to wait until the fumes had dissipated, which would take a few hours. Meanwhile because the tunnel was so narrow, the barges and the *Carn Ingli* would have to reduce the height of the boat so that it would fit through. In our case this meant dismantling the deck house. When all was ready we joined the queue and after a further few hours, until 3am in our case, we entered the tunnel and faced its menace, with Philip at the helm. After about three quarters of an hour, with great relief, we came out of the southern end of the tunnel and tied up. We looked back on the danger, real and symbolic, and had a short sleep until the opening of navigation.

Our route led us fairly steeply, for a canal, down to Dijon on the River Soane. To do this we had to pass through some forty-odd locks. This involved some hard work, but we did it with a will, and, aided by the early start, we tied up in Dijon in time for lunch in that pleasant city. The escargots were my choice. They were delicious and, in my memory, equalled only by those in Maison Jammet, Dublin.

Philip Castle

Now our journey entered another phase. We would leave the pretty byways, led by the little rivers and canals that drained into the Atlantic Ocean, and join the vast rivers which joined the great Rhone and the Mediterranean. The Rhone is not only broad, but in places fast flowing, with a strong current of up to nine knots. Here the barges were more powerful, needing to breast the nine knot current. So as well as a strong engine, they had a clipper bow which cut through the opposing current, throwing up a fine bow wave. We had been forewarned of the Rhone's swift currents, its swerving course, its evil rapids and shoals, and the wisdom of employing a Rhone pilot to make the descent of the lower river from Lyon to Avignon.

We had been recommended to use the reliable Kleber Lauriot, but learned at one of the locks that we passed through that he was already engaged. We carried on down the Soane through Lyon until we saw a smallish middle-aged man standing on a shingle bank facing the river. As we drew level he spoke out '*Je suis Albin Chechebacker, Pilote du Rhone*'. We took him on board immediately and Philip gave him the wheel. He steered the *Carn Ingli* across the confluence of the Soane and Rhone in a massive swooping curve quite unlike Philip's incisive course.

And now the journey entered a new phase at a new tempo. Albin Chechebacher was at the wheel for the next two days almost without cease. Every now and then he would point out a wrecked yacht stranded on a shingle bank and chant the mantra '*sans pilote, catastrophe*'. Meals were cursory and the day started as soon as navigation resumed. In my case I emerged on deck from the wheel house to see M. Chechebacher standing statuesque on a small mound, a mooring rope in his hand all prepared to cast off.

As the day went on we saw ahead of us an old ox-bow island over which hovered and soared a great assortment of raptors seeking their prey. We covered a surprising distance, from Lyon to Avignon under M. Chechebacher's pilotage until he left us at Avignon. From here on down the river was broad and placid, the banks covered in trees. Eventually we came to Port St.

Louis du Rhone, a sleepy commercial port. We made for the quay leading to a canal which would take us to the lower port and manoeuvred our approach which was going well until we ran aground and struck a mud bank. Full speed astern didn't help, so Philip ordered that we should lower the dinghy from the *Carn Ingli's* quarter, ship the tow-rope, make it fast and winch it from the boat, until the *Carn Ingli* majestically floated off the mud bank. We moored her further up stream. We slept well aboard and the next day considered our course. The one we settled on was to follow the coast eastwards along the Gulf de Lyon and the Côte d'Azur as far as Villefranche-sur-mer, cross over to Corsica, over to Sardinia, Sicily, to our winter base, Malta.

First we had to re-rig the boat, step the masts, fit the standing and bend on the sails. We did all this, not as well as our Royal Navy exemplars at Chichester Harbour, but at least it was a serviceable job. The next morning we woke to thick fog with the visibility down to one or two hundred yards. Philip elected to carry on as usual and we motored down the canal that connected the Bouches du Rhône river with the petro-chemical plant that bordered the Etang de Berre and our primary objective, the Mediterranean. Finally, we groped our way into the open sea.

The Carn Ingli

Chapter IV

THE CÔTE D'AZUR

We set a southerly course and kept a keen look out. We didn't see anything and thought that we probably were not on a sea lane. When we estimated that we were well clear of the coast, we checked the log reading and found that an easterly course would clear the headlands to the east of Toulon and put us close to the Isles d'Hyeres. By the time we came south of Toulon the fog had cleared, it was plain sailing and we were able to relax. We saw Toulon at the head of its inlet and passed on through the Isles d'Hyeres sound. Philip, who had sailed here before, quickly found a stern-on mooring and feeling very pieased with ourselves we enjoyed a *provençal* dinner and a good night's sleep.

Barry Laverty

Next morning Hyeres was shrouded with fog. We walked down the quay – the word 'brume' was on everyone's lips – but happily it did not last long and we sailed across to the little archipelago and found an anchorage in a wooded cove. I was anchor watch and fairly soon noticed under the clear water that the anchor was being towed backwards over hard corrugated sand. We re-anchored and all was well. We set off next morning with variable gentle breezes, heading eastwards in mellow sunshine. Soon there was a buzzing, swishing noise and we were overtaken by a motor launch driven by a beautiful amazon-like woman standing at the wheel. She was quite naked and looked neither to the right nor to the left. Gradually she disappeared into the distance and the image faded. Philip told Barry and I, who were apt to gape, that she had come from one of the islands which was a nudist colony.

Since the weather was fair and settled, we decided to anchor overnight at Tahiti Plage near St. Tropez. It looked very serene, but in fact turned out to be quite uncomfortable – the light swell proving to be greater than it had appeared to be and we rolled about and slept little all night. But this was a prelude to *La Dolce Vita*. We continued eastwards having a swim at midday – one of us staying aboard and trailing out the dinghy for fear of being caught out by an errant breeze of wind. No such wind troubled us. Barry produced a delicious lunch each day with a glass of rich *provençal* wine. If the wind defaulted by evening, as it often did, we motored into the next little port and presented ourselves to the Capitaine de Port and took up our allotted mooring, almost invariably stern on to the quay, which is the most convenient in the tideless Mediterranean.

Eventually the time came to leave and sail for the big Mediterranean islands, but first, two rituals were necessary, both cosmetic – one trivial, the other less so. The first was a hair cut for me, which was remarkable because it took so long. First the barber would walk around to one side of my head and select an already short hair, he would then cut a very short length off and then walk around to another short length of hair and repeat the process and so on *ad nauseam*. The net result, after the repetitive process was deemed to be complete, was scarcely perceptible, so I was glad to pay my bill and a handsome tip and unsteadily walk around Nice harbour where this tonsorial feat was performed.

The Carn Ingli

The second ritual was far more pragmatic: anti-fouling the *Carn Ingli*. Philip told us that it was essential now that we had come in from the temperate Atlantic waters to the warmer Mediterranean, our hull would be more vulnerable to marine growth, both zooitic: boring organisms, and botanic: profuse growths of seaweed.

The one rots the hull, the other tows a veritable inverted haystack around with it, slowing the boat down. So we sailed for the Port de la Darse at Villefranche-sur-mer. Here Philip, who as well as being a skipper of the *Carn Ingli,* was also its owner, negotiated the hire of a cradle on which the boat could be winched up onto the hard beside the harbour, under the branch of a delightful tree which gave shade to us while we repainted the top sides to give a clean fresh look. Here we painted on the anti-fouling below the water line. For this we used RNLI anti-fouling which Philip got from the previous owner. There was green or red. We hadn't enough of either, but we put it on anyway, leading to a spectacularly patchy appearance. Fortunately it didn't show much once the boat was re-launched. The same could not be said for my jeans on which I slopped anti-fouling so badly that they must have become an environmental hazard. So with these rituals performed, we enjoyed the interlude at Villefranche and its charming little restaurants and splendid wooded cliffs, and then set off on the new leg of our journey – crossing to Corsica.

Chapter V

CORSICA

Philip started our V8 engine for a preparatory warm-up before we left the harbour, as did our neighbours in the Port de la Darse who also were planning to leave. They gave their engines a short period of silky purring; but this did nothing to prepare us for the *Carn Ingli*'s awakening: it gave a sudden explosive roar following by a series of crackeling snarls and more of the explosive bangs which echoed back from the beautiful cliffs and elegant villas that backed the harbour. Barry and I tried to look the other way; Philip, on the other hand, nonchalantly manipulated the controls so that the engine gave even louder fits of bellowing. Eventually the din died down and we set course for Corsica.

The Carn Ingli

At this point Philip favoured making important crossings by night and making land fall somewhat before dawn. Hopefully this could mean that we could identify any lighthouse or buoy by its coded flashes, and possibly one or two co-ordinates as well. In the event we picked up the light of Calvi on the north-west coast, but it was still dark and Philip was reluctant to make a blind approach into the harbour. So again we adopted the ancient method of standing on and off well outside the harbour until dawn came, then we entered the harbour safely and dropped anchor well away from the quay as an anti-rat precaution. This meant that whenever we wanted to go ashore, we had to row there in the dinghy, but this was a pleasure rather than a nuisance. We would thread our way through the small craft on the anchorage, dividing our attention between the hazards of the harbour and the beauty of the surrounding mountains.

It turned out that we had plenty of time to look at them because the V-8 diesel had developed a fault on the way over from Calvi and we had to get a spare part over from England. This gave us plenty of time for swimming. I favoured walking around to the east side of Calvi to the sandy pine woods which were almost deserted and the water was clear. Barry was a catholic bather who enjoyed all conditions. Philip had eccentric views and practices in the water. He believed that it was quite wrong to jump in, dive or splash about, instead one should slither in gently and understand that the sea was more like jelly than a liquid. He particularly liked to bathe in the dark and lie on his back looking at the abundant Mediterranean stars.

Soon he had to abandon this and lie prone with his head in the engine under the deck house floor – his ample posterior monopolizing the deck house while he refitted the engine. He had a way with engines in the way that others have a way with horses. Philip had a stubbornness that seemed to say 'you will not defeat me, I will conquer you' and with this attitude bristling from him, rather than a love for machinery, he would bend it to his will. And so, after a struggle the engine was mended and we set course for Ajaccio, the capital of Corsica.

We put out of Calvi and set about making our offing in order to give ourselves plenty of sea room so that we would not be caught on the lee-shore. It was a bright sunny day, wind from the north, the sea a beautiful dark blue. We would swing around to the south west and in anticipation of this, Philip asked me to set the jib, the breeze was freshening and the swell increasing. I moved out to the foredeck and sat on the forepeak and began to hank on the jib. To my horror I suddenly saw a mountainous wave speeding towards us. It looked about the height of a double decker bus. Would it swamp us? Would it carry me away? I shouted 'Philip, Philip' and clung on, the sea began to rise and lifted me clear off the foredeck and swirled me around. I clung on tighter, the wave receded and deposited me back on the foredeck, facing forwards. I quickly checked whether there were any other horrors to come. There weren't, and I ran back to the deck house. 'Why do these freak waves occur?' None of us had a satisfactory answer. We carried on, the wind dropped abruptly, then it backed to south west. Strange, but then the Mediterranean is different from our familiar Atlantic. The wind settled in the south and we spent the rest of the day buffeted by its short chop and were glad to drop anchor in Ajaccio and row ashore to have a restorative drink on one of its comfortable terraces and enjoy the evening *paseo.*

Next day Barry and Philip settled into their familiar tasks, she to the boat-keeping, he to the tinkering with the engine. I didn't have any special work to do as deck hand and so took a day off. Swimming togs and the 1960 Bodley Head edition of *Ulysses* were all that I seemed to need. I caught the little blue bus along the northern side of the bay, got out at the edge of town and carried on walking out seaward until I came to a pleasant little beach where I had a swim. I think it was here that I really learned to swim. The water was a clear blue, warm but refreshing. I swam under the water, over the water, the crawl and the back stroke and stayed in as long as I wanted to, in contrast to the quick dip and desperate towelling that we had in our cold Irish waters. I spread my towel and lay in the sun until I was warm through and through; then got dressed and on the road again. I soon came to a little house with a garden and a few tables and chairs in front. I had lunch there in the company of a number of fairly docile wasps. I visited this place again and it didn't lose its magic.

The Carn Ingli

Chapter VI

Sardinia

Philip's tinkering reached a stage of resolution and we put to sea once more, this time we made for Bonifacio where the harbour is steep sided and circular and the entrance narrow. We climbed up through the little town on the inside of the circle and looked south over the rim. Across the rugged coast of the straights of Bonifacio we saw the bulk of Sardinia before us. Back down in the harbour the town was quiet, except for two English men loudly discussing the recent crisis in Africa. We invited them aboard and had a few drinks and the talk of Africa went on. Eventually we bade each other goodnight and we heard their voices passing from street to street proclaiming repeatedly 'Well Lamumba's had it'. This amused Barry greatly and quickly lulled us all to sleep.

The next morning we passed west to east through the strait of Bonifacio which was in a tranquil mood, unlike the interior of my head which was suffering from the agitations of the previous night. We carried on east about Sardinia and looked into Olbia's deep bay before anchoring in the shallow strait between l'Isola della Tavolara and the main island of Sardinia.

The weather was settled, fine and sunny with a steady breeze blowing from the north-west and we decided on plain sailing without the motor. There was quite a sea running and the *Carn Ingli* rolled about, giving away any pretensions at being a stiff sailor, nevertheless it was very pleasant to watch the waves skim and bounce, driven by the moderate breeze.

Later the wind shifted to the south-west. There were fires lit on some of the low hills and plumes of smoke drifted up the coast. We kept on sailing south along the sparsely populated coast until fatigue and the sudden onset of dusk made us look for an anchorage.

Shortly after we raised Capo Carbonara we saw between two small capes, a sandy cove with a little house at its head. A sharp land breeze blew down it. We motored in and inspected the sandy bottom. It looked ok. The bower and kedge was Philip's verdict. We laid each anchor carefully, but we were not experts. We slept well, but awoke to a fierce tangle of chain and cordage, which took a long time to put to rights, a lesson painfully learned.

On leaving the little bay we met a smart looking coaster. She was making for Capo Carbonara and neatly slipped through the strait between headland and island. We promptly followed such an exemplar, but our V8 began to cough occasionally. Uneasily we reminded ourselves that we could sail in to Cagliari, our next port of call. The unease grew as we remembered the old saying 'the wind never blew anyone back to Cagliari', published in no less a shrine than the *Admiralty Pilot*.

Such a thought was too much for our main sail. A small tear appeared in its leech and very soon it tore in half. Ruefully we pulled it down and stowed it in its sail bag. That left a jib and a mizzen and an ailing engine whose fits and starts became more erratic. It grew dark. Harbour and navigation lights were turned on. We limped in, and were given a good berth, next to a small naval vessel. Tomorrow would be another day.

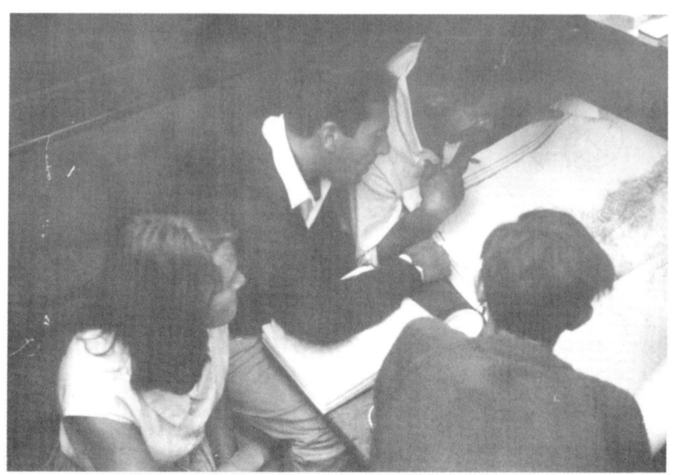

Barry, Bruno (a local lecturer they befriended), Philip and Pat, Cagliari

Fresh bread and coffee saw us on the move again. We soon found a sail makers in a street just off the quay. As deck hand it fell to my lot to carry the heavy cotton sail. We folded it up neatly and I carried it on my head. I felt immensely proud of my burden, though no-one seemed to take the least notice of it. It was spread out over the chandler's wooden counter, though only a small part would fit, and most spilled out over the floor. There followed an impassioned discussion, or rather monologue, mainly conducted by the young woman who was going to make the repair. She frequently repeated the words '*questi, qui*' whilst waggling a clump of sail cloth in the air. I hadn't the remotest idea at that time what either the words or gestures meant and neither did my friends, we all being as ignorant of Italian as of French. Eventually through repetition and sign language in which the women were the more skillful, an accord was reached, and we went back to the boat feeling that at least one small step had been taken in its repair.

Our two main sources of power had been put out of action and we spent almost a month putting things to rights again. Philip found, after much rummaging that the engine water pump had become defective and again a replacement from England had to be fitted.

The *Carn Ingli* became something of a landmark in the harbour. Young and old visited it. Prominent amongst the oldsters was the retired skipper of a yacht owned by a local nobleman. The old skipper and his entourage visited daily. He expressed surprise that a group so inexpert as ours should venture on such a major voyage and I dare say he was right. Our other group of visitors were younger and more light-hearted. They whisked us off by car to Poetta where there was a fine beach and swimming.

Before leaving London I had read in one of the English papers of a bus in Sardinia being held up at gunpoint and the passengers being robbed. The tone was that it was a curiosity rather than a frequent happening, but nevertheless it put one in the *qui vive.*

Cagliari was hardly a beautiful town, but it had its colourful aspects. Every so often a herd of maybe thirty or forty horses would be driven through the streets. The horsemen wore blue jackets, riding boots and carried whips and their destination was the harbour from which they were no doubt exported.

It was late in the season and we needed to be off. We will aim for Marsala on the western extremity of Sicily. If we should miss it and sail too northerly or too southerly a course, we could add hundreds of miles to our journey. If we get it right the crossing will be approximately 200 miles.

Pat, Bruno, Barry and Philip at Cagliari

Chapter VII

SICILY

As luck would have it we had an easy passage from Cagliari and made our landfall in the Egadi archipelago which we raised dead ahead, not without a certain degree of smugness. This is better known as the big toe of Italy and a wild, remote, rugged place it is, where the Tyrrhenian Sea meets the Sicillian Channel. Our passage was marked by two presents; one a copy of *A Portrait of the Artist as a Young Man*. Our friend Carlo put out in a motor launch into the Golfo de Cagliari, caught up with us, and handed us, across the waves, a copy of Joyce's great work. The second, if I may be a little fanciful, was also a present from the sea. This time it came at the end of our voyage when the night watch woke us on the sea in the magnificent Edagi Islands. Strewn over the deck were enough flying fish to make a lavish breakfast for all three of us. During the night we had heard them whirring over the boat, sometimes colliding with the superstructure. I quickly collected them up and Barry fried them with oil and lemon. They were like fresh mackerel. The perfect present.

Our anchorage in deep water between islands and mountain was, to say the least of it, exposed, and we prudently withdrew to Marsala where there was a well-sheltered harbour and scattering of small craft.

The next morning we woke to a sirocco, a south east wind at first from the dry desert, later becoming humid and sandy and blowing half a gale. We saw one intrepid yachtsman running before it and were told that it was excellent for getting places. Malta and laying up for the winter were our current ambitions, so we stayed in harbour. We were kept there for four days while the sirocco blew itself out.

Eating at Marsala was not a very exciting experience. The dining room of the hotel was austere, the spaghetti no less so. Perhaps there was now a touch of the jaded gourmand in us. We still had about two hundred miles to sail, so better to get on with it. We sailed along the south coast of Sicily meeting the occasional trawler, its single cylinder diesel engine giving a booming 'thump thump', and producing an exotic catch, always including *triglia* red mullet, which became a staple diet, bought on the steps of the quay.

We called in at Sciacca. Darkness was falling early now and we arrived in the dark. The market was in full swing and the square was lit by flares made by rushes held by iron brackets in the walls. On to the next day with the mountains around Agrigento to our north, and Licata, our next port of call, ahead. A rough town, short on the niceties – a young man squatting to defecate in the gutter. Date of latest treatment with D.D.T. chalked on the wall, the men hissing to attract Barry's attention or to solicit cigarettes '*cigarretta, cigarretta, cigarretta*'.

The last day, we turn out bows to the south and make for the Malta Channel between Sicily and Malta. We meet a British naval cruiser, it makes its way westwards. Philip dips our ensign. A sailor runs from the bows to stern of the cruiser to return our salute, a bit tardy, but the courtesy was observed. We leave the small island of Gozo astern, and the gleaming city of Valletta, the final destination of this trip, is ahead, a far cry from Birdham Lock, Chichester Harbour.

The End

Appendix I:

Later Shipmates

The following year the journey continued, and new visitors on the *Carn Ingli* included Pauline Bewick, Nuala O'Faolain and Peter Murray.

Philip Castle and Peter Murray

Philip Castle, Pauline Bewick, Peter Murray

Barry Laverty, Nuala O'Faolain, Pauline Bewick

Barry Laverty, Nuala O'Faolain, Pauline Bewick

After selling the Carn Ingli, Philip bought a catamaran

Appendix II:

CHARACTER SKETCHES OF THE THREE FRIENDS

Pat at Mucksna Lodge, Kenmare, 1954

Like my shipmates Barry and Philip, I was a habitué of No 51 Frankfurt Avenue, Dublin and knew both of them well before we started sailing together. '51' was presided over by Harry Bewick who let out inexpensive rooms to students. It had an unofficial status as an alternative college. The focal point was the sitting room on the first floor at the front. The windows were large and sunny and in the winter there was an open fire. The ethos was bohemian and there was an almost permanent philosophical seminar going on, all quite un-selfconscious and spontaneous. Another of our influences was John Watling of University College,

London who visited outside term times. Originally a student of psychoanalysis, he had become a linguistic analysist.

My father was Irish, originally from Roscommon, and my mother was from a Liverpool sea-faring family. She was a teacher of geography and I probably owe her my life-long interest in geography, history, archaeology and the natural world.

I was a medical student at Trinity and for some time lived in college which I liked immensely. But the medical course is a long one, and many of my friends moved on; I moved too, but in a different direction. I went to live in '51' and at the same time developed an interest in psychiatry. At that time it was necessary to move abroad and I opted for London where I enrolled in the external course in the Institute of Psychiatry at the Maudesley Hospital and the Institute of Neurology at Queen Square. I worked at clinical psychiatry at Tooting Bec Hospital and St Ebba's Hospital, Epsom and took a personal interest in dream analysis.

Pat skiing at Gargellan, Austria, 1963

In 1963 Pauline Bewick and I married and returned to Ireland. Here I got a joint appointment at Dean Swift's and St Patrick's Hospital, Dublin and also at Trinity College in teaching and research; student health, and psychotherapy. While 'on call', I started drawing and, in the 1960s, had art accepted into the Exhibition of Living Art, the National Exhibition of Graphic Art and shown on RTÉ television.

In 1966 our first daughter Poppy was born, followed in 1970 by Holly. We moved to County Kerry in 1973 and settled in a remote valley at Caragh Lake. I have sailed three small boats since the *Carn Ingli* days. I worked at Killarney psychiatric hospital until 1996 and since retiring have enjoyed skiing and horse riding and re-engaging in creative pursuits, most particularly oil painting and writing.

Pat Melia and Pauline Bewick with family; Holly and daughters Ciara and Giada; Poppy and sons Aran and Adam, photographed by Nina Finn-Kelcey in 2005

Barry with her mother Maura, father Jim and brother Jimmy

Barry did virtually no painting in the National College of Art and Design and probably spent as much time at Pauline Bewick's house, 51 Frankfurt Avenue, as she did at the College. Barry and Pauline were best friends from the age of fifteen when they first met at art school and their mothers also became friends. Her family lived nearly, her mother was Maura Laverty, a famous writer, and her father worked in *The Irish Times*. She was also influenced by the people of '51', and fell in love briefly with Troy Kennedy-Martin and John Watling. She had a long shiny ponytail, and wore expensive angora sweaters which accentuated her beauty.

In the 1960s her mother Maura and brother Jimmy died. Their illnesses and deaths grieved her. A change took place over Barry; her relationship with Philip became closer. Later she started to write poems and to paint pictures in a bright colourful style. Both Barry and Philip had a long period of artistic production; Barry, painting and writing and Philip painting. At times they collaborated on the same canvas, with Philip painting the buildings and Barry the people. She wrote and illustrated *Cooking for Cats* (Methuen 1985) and illustrated *Cry Wolf*, a collection of Aesop's Fables (Methuen 1988), and Maura Laverty's books *The Cottage in the Bog* (Townhouse, 1990) and *The Queen of Aran's Daughter* (Poolbeg, 1995).

They both successfully exhibited at the Portal Gallery, London and lived most usually at Villefranche-sur-mer and in the Monti di Chianti area of Italy where they bought a *casa colonica* at Bricciano. There they had a lot of friends and had frequent and memorable dinner parties. Barry was incredibly generous, just like her mother. She gave painting classes in the Burren and shared her art knowledge openly. She particularly loved living in Bricciano and indeed introduced the Bewick-Melia family to it in 1972. She was self-sufficent and very practical; when a stone wall needed to be built at Bricciano, rather than wait for builders, she did it herself. It still stands perfectly. Barry created food over an open fire and was an amazing cook – no doubt encouraged by her mother's book, *Full and Plenty*.

Barry Laverty, 1950s

Barry Castle with some of her paintings

Philip and Barry outside the Portal Gallery, London

I met Philip first sometime in the early 1950s when we were both students at Trinity College. He studied physics, called experimental science in those days. He soon dropped out of college as he didn't like all the mathematics. Before Trinity he had done a course at the Aeronautical College at Loughborough in England. His father had bought him a wind tunnel to help him with his studies, and for recreation he had a maroon Porsche sports car.

His appearance was eccentric. He was rather portly, wore a crumpled tweed suit and a tweed hat and carried a baggy umbrella. He was jolly, knowledgeable and fond of making puns. He had a small sailing boat, a one tonner, which he evidently used to sail about Chichester Harbour, the Spithead and the Solent.

His first visual interest was splendidly ambitious – to make an animated cartoon. To get over the tedious animation he painted his figures on microscope slides and moved them about with tiny electric motors. The first one that I saw showed a Dublin classical terrace. The camera travels along the length of it and reveals that a front door has opened and there looking out is an ape. With almost infinite patience Philip built some characters and a narrative and, to his amazement, this animated cartoon was shown at the National Film Theatre, London.

In 1963 Barry and Philip married and settled in four principal residences where they completed their life's work. Philip's favourite home was at Villefranche-sur-mer overlooking the sea. There was also a studio in South Kensington and the old metal workshop at the Elephant and Castle which originally housed his family's factory where old-fashioned deep-sea diving helmets were made, the source of the Castle family wealth.

Philip became a full-time painter. His subjects were almost invariably town or city scapes with only occasional groups of people shown usually engaged in some quirkish activity. His towns and cities are magnificently painted with oils on canvas, large with lots of detail. An idiosyncratic perspective and ebullient sense of fun have led to the classification of 'primitive'. To some extent this is justified, but in fact, Philip's paintings are highly sophisticated and his colouring a complete delight.

He enjoyed the cinema and food, though as life went on he became more and more interested in his paintings. His old age was marred by a debilitating illness and, instead of it, I like to remember him in his prime, at the dinner table, expounding one of his extraordinary theories with great enthusiasm.

Philip and Barry at Bricciano, Italy

Appendix III

'Some Queer Hawks': A Family Memoir

Chapter I

THE CONNAUGHT QUEEN

Let us give the Connaught Queen three of her names: Grainne Ó Maille; Grace O'Malley; Granuaile and add that she was an Irish Queen, widely known as the Pirate Queen. She lived during the latter part of the sixteenth century. Her two castles stood on either side of the entrance to the spacious, island-studded waters of Clew Bay: one on Achill Island, the other on Clare Island. The castles were not grand affairs such as are met with in the wealthier parts of Europe, but simple towers, not too high, built on a rectangular base.

Within Queen Grace's tribe of O'Malleys, in the Irish, Ó Maille, is a smaller sept: the Melias, Irish Ó Maele. It will be the doings of these latter that will be the subject of my memoirs of the Irish side of our family. The O'Malleys were one of the quite numerous tribes or clans of the west of Ireland. Galway is known as the City of the Tribes.

I believe that her ships were galliots which were small galleys, having a single mast and sail. They could be sailed down wind or rowed up wind by sixteen or twenty oars-men. This gave them a great advantage for piracy as it enabled them to attack from any point of the compass, including from down wind. The last would be particularly dangerous for a lightly armed victim who could make no escape up wind. But probably Granny Imallye, as Sir Philip Sidney chose to call her, preferred a relatively comfortable protection business with perhaps a little espionage to eek out funds, rather than a bloody showdown. Her fleet with their bases in Clare Island and Achill Island gave her untrammelled cruising grounds between Galway Bay and Erris Head along the west coast of Ireland, and was the base for forays as far away as North Africa and Scandinavia.

In an Irish clan or tribe at this period of Irish history, while the head of the tribe was acknowledged, the land that they occupied was communally held, thus giving the individual tribe members a secure status.

Despite or because of Grainne's extensive lands in the west and dominion over the western sea board, not everyone recognized her as Queen. The Lord Deputy, Queen Elizabeth's man in Connacht, didn't and, as a recent appointee, was particularly zealous in establishing British rule throughout the province, harrying Queen Grainne at every opportunity. So Grainne hatched a plan: she would go to the top and petition Queen Elizabeth herself.

A ship, or possibly a small fleet was made ready, and set forth probably taking the southabout course down the west coast of Ireland, rounding Mizzen Head, crossing the Irish Sea, sailing up the Channel, rounding the North foreland and sweeping up the Thames Estuary to anchor below London Bridge. Probably intrigued to meet such an intrepid woman, Elizabeth granted Grainne a general audience. One version of the story tells us that the Pirate Queen was as usual barefooted for the occasion, more insist that she would have worn her finest clothes, all agree that her bow was of precisely the same depth as that of Elizabeth as they greeted one another. It is historical fact that her petition was granted, and the Lord Deputy was forced to be more circumspect, at least for a while. Elizabeth seems to have had a soft spot for Grainne. As well as granting her petition, on another occasion she capped all by pardoning her from the gallows in a dramatic last minute scene.

They were after all in the same business, especially as Elizabeth had recently accepted Sir Francis Drake's stupendous profit from piracy in the Pacific. The anecdote which I think most reveals Grainne's character concerns a pinch of snuff. Elizabeth had evidently noticed Grainne's voracious snuff habit and seeing her become agitated when her supply ran out at a reception, saw to it that a little embroidered handkerchief laden with snuff was made up and slipped to her. Grainne accepted it unconcernedly, snorted it all over the place, and then threw it in the fire.

And so back to Ireland, but the adventures were by no means over. She decided to return for some unknown reason via Howth, a fishing and ferry port north of Dublin which was and still is the home of the Earl of Howth. Grainne was used to the lavish hospitality that was customary in the west of Ireland, and set out to Lord Howth's residence without an invitation fully confident of a warm welcome and a convivial evening. When she was not admitted through the gates she was outraged by what she considered, with some justification, an insult. We know that Queen Grainne was a woman of action and now she excelled herself. Next morning her crew kidnapped Lord Howth's young son and informed the distraught father that his son would be restored to him only if the Earl agreed to the following conditions; the gate of Howth Demesne should never be closed and secondly an extra place at dinner for an unexpected guest should always be laid. Recently I was introduced to a member of the Earl's household and was assured that on special occasions such as at

Christmas and other holidays, Queen Grainne's conditions are still observed and we trust that this will be continued for many centuries to come.

Chapter II

The Clipper Captain

Captain William Inglis has the distinction of having a whole chapter devoted to him in Andrew Shewan's book *The Great Days of Sail*, but Third Mate Shewan's chapter is far from flattering. It is titled "How it was Not Done" and taxes Captain Inglis with timidity and excessive caution and habitually arriving with the cargo of black tea somewhat late in the season. Mr Shewan was a devotee of the popular belief that first boat home, best price. It was certainly exciting for mid-Victorians to read in the morning paper over breakfast of the arrival of the clippers in the chops of the channel. But did this mean that the clippers first home were the most profitable? More likely it was a naïve romantic view which ignored pragmatic matters such as the selection of the best teas on offer by the Chinese junk captains who brought the tea down river to the mouth of the Kowloon River where the clippers were moored.

It was here that the middle men, or in some cases the clipper captains, eagerly awaited them to make keen bargains for the best quality tea. Then came the voyage home, down the shallow shoal waters and pirate ridden South China Sea, important to outsail the pirate junks here and to avoid running aground. Then westward across the Indian Ocean around the Cape of Good Hope to cross the Equator and home on the Westerlies. Plenty of time to meet up with a storm or two.

The skippers bent on making a fast passage could run into trouble here. Cracking on at speed in foul weather throws great strain on the crew, sails and spars. On the famous "Cutty Sark" a man, John Francis, was lost from the rigging in these circumstances, the second such occurrence of the voyage. Their shipmates mutineered for three days, making it clear that they would not put up with being driven so dangerously anymore. Less serious but nevertheless significant damage could be done: torn sails, broken spars, parted ropes that would not have enhanced the profit and loss account sheets. The canny, hard-headed Scots' syndicates who employed Captain Inglis would not have been impressed by such extravagances. His less phrenetic pace suited the crew as well as the owners, and my great grandfather, who I feel the need to vindicate, had no difficulty in recruiting a crew of the best sea men for the next voyage. In it he made sure that there was included a fiddler to give the men music and dancing between the dog watches.

I first heard of him from my mother, daughter of William Fleming Inglis, a chief engineer in the Liverpool Booth Line fleet. She mentioned casually that we had a forebear who was a clipper captain and pointed to a coral necklace, which she was wearing, saying that he had brought it back for her from the islands. I heard no more of him until I was browsing through Hodges Figgis bookshop in Dublin where I came across Shewan's book, flipped through it and my great grandfather's name leapt from the page at me.

William Inglis was probably born around 1820 and spent his early years in Aberdeen, Scotland, a sea port heavily engaged in the whaling trade. The books which mention him and are known to me give no information as to his early life, though curiously again I unexpectedly came across "William Inglis" in print.

This time in a biography of Lord Cochrane, the swash buckling dare devil of the Napoleonic Wars, who was the template for the fictional Jack Aubrey of Patrick O'Brian's Aubrey/Maturin novels.

With peace came unemployment for Lord Cochrane which was, however, terminated by the offer of command of the Brazilian Navy. In it he was glad to join a cadre of English and Scottish officers, amongst whom is listed Lieutenant William Inglis. The entry in the appendix expands his name to William James Inglis. All three names are common in Scotland and there may be no connection between him and our William Inglis, but I like to think of my mother's choice of the name James for one of our cats indicates a link. This cat's full name was James Edward. Edward was his patronym following the Irish custom; my mother, never one to be outdone, quite likely supplied a name from the distaff, hence James Edward who gave birth to many a litter of tabby kittens and I hope burgeons the case for consanguinuity between the two Williams. Here you may notice I have my tongue slightly in my cheek. There would of course have been a generation gap between the Lieutenant and the Captain.

William Inglis' first command was *The Gauntlet*, an extremely elegant ship bearing the great sails which preceded the horizontally divided ones of the later clippers. It was designed for the run to Australia on which it carried passengers and for them had such luxuries as water showers. But that did not last too long and she was transferred to the tea trade.

Quite soon he made a passage that should have laid to rest the ghost of timidity and the inability to sail his ship fast. In October 1856 he drove *The Gauntlet* before the North East monsoon the length of the South China

Sea from Whampoa to Anjer in six days to equal Captain Freeman's record established the year before and not bettered by a clipper since. In 1863 Captain Inglis was made Master of *The Black Prince*, a brand new clipper of which much was expected. Inglis, still in his physical prime, responded with the season's fastest passage from China to England: Hong Kong to Liverpool in only ninety-three days.

Inglis continued in the tea trade for sixteen seasons adopting his favoured mode, not driving his men, his boat or himself too hard and keeping his employers in handsome profit. He evidently was an impressive figure endowed with a Roman nose and who responded to any criticism with rapid sarcasm. He entertained dinner parties ashore with accounts of his exploits that Shewan claims would rival Alexander himself and apparently masked the cautious reality.

Shewan, his Third Mate and stern critic, tells two stories exemplifying his character and with them we will bid goodbye to Captain William. In the first we see him anchored off a narrow sound between two large islands through which he must pass. He is pacing the quarter deck agonizing over whether he should go ahead on the gentle breeze which would carry him through the sound, or might drop and leave him without steerage way in restricted water half way through. Two decrepit vessels come down and pass easily through the channel leaving our hero still at anchor on his splendid clipper ship still racked by the dilemma. Now we shift from minor to major key. Inglis had as one of his mates an officer of considerable experience, perhaps not matched by great accomplishment. This does not prevent him from sharing with his fellow officers many a story of brilliant feats of seamanship achieved by him on his previous appointments, particularly when sailing under the Canadian flag and he lets it be known that all was done much better than under the present command. Captain Inglis bides his time until on a sweltering evening a black, dark cloud swells on the western horizon, its edges orange and violet. We hear rumbling of thunder, and flashes of lightening spear the rapidly swelling cloud. A crisis is imminent. Inglis approaches the Canadian and announces that he is going below and instructs him to take over the ship. As he disappears the storm breaks and the poor old officer is overwhelmed by a mass of backed desperately flapping sails and whipping ropes. After twenty minutes of chaos Captain Inglis steps out of his cabin and quickly restores order. We hear no more glorious stories from the unhappy mate.

Despite his earlier strictures Shewan ends his chapter on an affectionate note 'Good old Inglis! There was many a worse'.

Chapter III

THE CHIEF ENGINEER

My maternal grandfather, William Fleming Inglis, was born about 1855, much about the time when his father sailed the clipper ship *Gauntlet* on a sea of spray from Whampoa to Anjer in six days driven by the north east monsoon. William Fleming Inglis was also to have a career on the sea. Perhaps not such a romantic one as his father, it was one which marked the change from sail to steam. W. F. Inglis was born in Aberdeen and spent his early life there until he went to Merseyside to train as a Marine Engineer. His first step was to become apprenticed to Camel Lairds, the famous ship builders at Birkenhead. On occasional trips by bus to Liverpool, I remember seeing their giant cranes thrusting out from a jumble of sheds to dominate the skyline, and behind them the fast flowing tides breasted by the tug-like ferry boats churning the brown polluted waters of the river Mersey. His apprenticeship completed, he joined the Liverpool based Booth Line and eventually became a chief engineer on one of their ships.

Their principal run was from Liverpool to the mouth of the Amazon and thence two and a half thousand miles up the great river to Iquitos in Peru. Iquitos is in the upper Amazon rain forest and at this time was a boom town. It had an opera house – Caruso sang there. Meanwhile the stevedores loaded rubber from the vast jungle into the holds of the dingy, black funneled Booth Line steamers. Plastic had not yet been invented and rubber was much in demand. The round trip from Liverpool must have been at least twelve thousand miles, half of them through steaming jungle full of rampant tropical disease. What sort of man could endure such a life?

Photographs of him on the deck together with the Captain and another ship's officer show him in a rather shabby uniform, his engine room gear no doubt, but nevertheless he manages considerable panache. He was a little below medium height and like other nineteenth century Inglis's had an imposing roman nose. My mother told me with a tinge of amusement that in his heyday he had been a lady's man. Whatever else about him he had stickability; he carried on working in the Booth Line until shortly after World War I.

Recently I was walking along Upper Bridge Street in Killorglin, our local town, when I saw a handsome sea chest for sale on the pavement outside Mary Callaghan's antique shop. The chest bore a label on which was painted in large letters "BOOTH LINE" and the names of two sea or river ports in a language I guessed to be portugese. I mentioned this to Madeleine Crowley, a friend of our family, who put it into a computer search. To our surprise she came across the name Daniel Mulvihill whom it told us was with the Booth Line as a Radio Officer from 1915 to 1919. He was a Killorglin man and a contemporary of my grandfather. The Booth Line was a small one and they may well have been shipmates. Be that as it may, my son-in-law Conor Mulvihill is the grandnephew of Radio Officer Daniel Mulvihill and Conor is crew on my little boat at Kells Bay – we are shipmates.

After World War I, W. F. Inglis was chosen to be chief engineer on a German boat which was awarded to Australia as reparation for losses incurred so he made the long journey out, noting that "the hottest place in the world is the Red Sea with a following wind".

Grandfather Inglis retired from the Booth Line in the early 1920s and by way of a less arduous job became chief engineer on the Irish Lights boat. This was a handsome little craft which serviced the Irish lighthouses and light-vessels. Once a year the Commissioners of the Irish Lights went on a cruise in order to make an inspection from their trim boat craft with its light-grey hull and biscuit-coloured funnel. Champagne was consumed and the atmosphere was like that of a Gilbert and Sullivan light opera.

He, my grandfather, lived until eighty-four and often came to our house and stayed for long periods, as was the custom with relatives in those times. He wore a dapper navy-blue suit, a winged collar, tie, waist-coat with watch chain, and, out of doors, a bowler hat and stick. At home as he walked about the house he sang to himself *"Two lovely black eyes"* meaning beautiful eyes rather than bruised; and something that sounded like *"Hey, Diddlesome dee …"* but did not seem to have any conclusion. He was quite active and each morning walked the three miles down to Wrexham where he took a cup of coffee at Philips Café and thence back for dinner at half past one. He was a martinet at meal times, rapping the table with the haft of his knife to bring my brother and me to order, at other times quite jovial he would compliment us on our abilities as trenchermen.

My favourite recollection is of him standing on his bunk on the B & I night boat from Liverpool to Dublin. He has opened the port hole and his head is out of it scanning the sea traffic and buoys lit by white, green and red lights. Every now and then he draws his head in and explains to us our progress towards and over the Mersey bar. Time and tide had not dulled his love of the sea.

Chapter IV

The Hedge Teacher, The Merchants and Others

Family tradition has it that my father's grandfather was called Patrick and lived in the country to the south-west of Roscommon town. He lived in the early to middle part of the nineteenth century, farmed land and was a hedge school teacher. He held his school at Slaveen, behind the white thorn hedge there, to the west of the County Home.

He sent his son, Edward, who had been born in 1846, during the famine, into the town to enter into commerce and make money. This he did very handsomely owning a thriving grocery business in the centre of town. As well as supplying the town and surrounding country, he sold tea wholesale throughout the west of Ireland. Edward and his wife had eleven children and it was a busy household. It was usual for over twenty to sit down to dinner which was taken in the middle of the day and included the household workers. At this time a housemaid earned as little as twelve shillings and sixpence a year, but as well got her all-important keep.

There were three sons and eight daughters. Life was not all work. The menfolk enjoyed fishing, shooting and racing and in the summer rented a house beside Lough Ree which was near to the town. The father got a boat made in Lanesborough. It was considered rather luxurious with copper fastened larch planking. The boat-maker had a man deliver it by rowing it from Lanesborough to Galey Bay, no mean distance. My grandfather grew rich in the way that country merchants did, and, as was the tradition, bought up small farms around the town. In less sensible moments he bought a few race horses. They were entered for the Roscommon Races which were raced to rules. My father told me that before the race the horses were given a liberal feed of whiskey. This was no shifty felony on the part of Ned Melia, but a regular, even essential part of the proper preparation of a race horse for his work and indeed he was rewarded when the horse came in second in the big race.

My grandfather Ned described himself as a merchant in the various certificates he had to sign. At least this was so in Ireland. In England it was modified to the less dashing "Provisions Merchant". Perhaps the English clerks didn't want him getting any notions that he was a gentleman.

My father was the eldest son in the family of eleven. His mother's wish for him was the priesthood and after four years in Maynooth he graduated in Latin and Greek, but that was the end of Maynooth's and Paddy Melia's relationship; theirs' was a mésalliance. He qualified as a doctor at the National University of Ireland in Dublin and spent his working life in a coal-mining village at Summerhill near Wrexham, where he married William Fleming Inglis's daughter, Edith and had two sons, Bill and I.

My brother and I adored our uncle Joe, who was the baby of the family. He stayed with us for about a year on his way back from Europe at the beginning of World War II. He could take ailing clocks to bits and reassemble them, shoot a football with stinging force, whack long drives at golf, do a swallow or jackknife dive from the top board at Blackrock, and evidently enjoyed our company. Joe had set out on a career as a naval architect at Vickers at Newcastle-upon-Tyne. He was amused to announce that the acme of his achievement was to design the interior of the third-class bar of a transatlantic liner. Further progress was halted by pulmonary tuberculosis. Anti-tubercular drugs were not yet available and he had a pulmonectomy and recuperated in Leysin in Switzerland. He liked life on the Continent. He skied with the local young men, spoke French with a bizarre accent driven by his Roscommon drawl, and formed a liaison with Blanche, an assistant of Coco Chanel. They were to have opened a branch for Chanel in Zurich, but Hitler's advance stopped that. Uncle Joe caught the last plane from Paris and came to stay at Summerhill. He continued to correspond with Blanche who had married during the war. His collection of her letters was terminated by an envelope with a black border around 1960. Blanche had died. After Joe's death, I found by his bedside an old photograph of her reclining in an alpine meadow.

Aunt Bridie married into the Waldron family who had a large shop in Ballyhaunis, thus uniting the two business houses in Roscommon and Mayo. Milo, one of Bridie's sons described Ballyhaunis lyrically; set in meadows, at night loud with corncrakes coming right up to the backs of the town's houses. Milo was a sports reporter on the *Irish Independent*.

Kathleen, in religion Mother Ignatious, another of my aunts joined the Loreto Order of nuns and taught french in their schools in and around Dublin. Another aunt joined a convent of a more humble type at Castlerea. She gave my wife, Pauline Bewick and I a beautiful embroidered table cloth which she had made herself as a wedding present.

Daisy married John Mulhall, a bank manager in Boyle. His mother was a Macdermot, one of whom is the Prince of Coolavin. The latter is an island in nearby

Lough Key. The prince works in a financial house in the City of London and as well as being descended from the ancient kings of Ireland has a literary distinction. Anthony Trollope gave his first novel the title of *The Macdermots of Ballycloran*. It is about an ancient pre-colonial Irish family already impoverished, and living in a dilapidated big house somewhere on the Leitrim-Roscommon border; so that allowing for literary license, there are similarities. I attended John Mulhall's funeral, as did quite a number of the Macdermot family. At first I thought that they were family retainers as their clothing struck me as old fashioned, but closer observation showed a rather dashing eccentricity and their accents and conversation seemed cultured and animated and I'm sorry that I never met them again.

When Edward Melia died in 1918, all the unattached members of the family moved to a house in Anglesea Road, Ballsbridge, Dublin. Eileen was as deaf as a post and probably paranoid. After her only outing of the week, which she took with the small drove of Melias to Mass, she locked herself into her room, not to emerge for another week. It was difficult to communicate with her because of her deafness and in emergencies a note had to be slipped under her door in the hope that she would see it sooner rather than later.

One of my aunts had an unexpected death. She ate a lobster for her lunch at a café in Grafton Street and very quickly developed ptomaine poisoning and died. Neither Florry nor Eva married though they were both charming and good looking.

The matrilineal family was the Taylors. For commercial reasons they based themselves on either side of the Irish Sea: in Armagh and in Liverpool. In

Armagh they raised cattle which they drove on the hoof to the Liverpool cattle boat, and marketed in Liverpool. Grandmother Taylor met Grandpa Inglis there and married her, taking her to his sea-farer's home. My mother's cousins the Chadburns kept a ship's chandlers there in that vast port. One of them invented and patented the ship's telegraph which enabled the ship's officers to ring down orders from the bridge to the engine room requiring the engineers to give half speed ahead, full speed ahead, half speed astern *et cetera*. Nearly all ships had one in the steam age.

Roy Chadburn gave my parents a travelling clock for their wedding present. It was still in use when my parents died sixty years later.

My maternal grandmother spent her early years in Armagh before she crossed the Irish Sea. I remember her telling a story of an eagle plucking a baby from its pram and flying off to the mountains to devour it. Were there still eagles in the Mourne Mountains in her time, or was this part of a familial timidity? If the latter it didn't seem to affect my mother much. She was a spirited go-ahead affectionate woman. She attended Liverpool University where she studied geography. She also went to lectures in the English School given by the brilliant Professor Compagniac. After graduating she considered staying on as a post-graduate and writing a thesis on coastal erosion, but for some reason did not persist with this. Instead she took up teaching and accepted a post in the splendidly named Giggleswick College in the Northern Pennines. She made two abiding friends there, each complimenting an important facet of her own nature. Elsa Bedwell was devoted to the open air life. She was an alpinist and had her own guide, Zippert, from Pontresina. She started her climbing career in the Edwardian era and I remember her describing how little balls of snow used to stick to the hem of her long tweed skirt. Gertie Fishwick was a cultured intellectual whose home was in Hampstead Garden suburb whence she made the journey to the frigid North Country at the beginning of each term. She fostered my mother's love of the theatre which she indulged on trips to London where she would stay with Gertie and visit the West End theatres. Her favourite plays were Shakespeare's and her favourite actor John Gielgud.

My mother and father used often join the Bedwells in the Alps, especially at Interlaken in the Bernese Oberland and would climb with her as far as the base hut. Then Elsa would carry on for the summit whilst my parents and Frank, Elsa's clergyman husband, would descend to the comforts of the valley.

Uncle Will was my mother's younger brother, good natured and serious-minded. Before World War I he laboured to win a scholarship at Oxford and got one by adopting the strategy of ignoring the examination instructions and answering only one of the set questions and showing the depth and scope of his knowledge. He was barely ensconced in Jesus College when World War I broke out. His mentor now advised him not to apply for a commission as the life-span of a young officer in the trenches was so abysmally short, and so he spent the war as a non-commissioned officer. His job became the mechanic in charge of the horn which sounded warning of the release of poisonous gas from the German lines. His moment of glory came when his horn broke down and no longer gave a warning. He placed the reserve horn in a wheel barrow and walked out across the maelstrom of bullets in no-man's land heading for a good place to re-install it, virtually certain of altruistic suicide. The

Germans quickly saw what was going on and gallantly ceased fire to enable him to finish his job, which he did. He was offered a mention in dispatches or, as an alternative, two weeks leave at home. He chose the latter.

Back at Oxford after the war he was invited to breakfast at a fellow student's rooms. He lit a cigarette towards the end of the meal which drew from his host an enquiry as to whether the aroma of his bacon was interfering with his guest's enjoyment of the cigarette. The host had been too young for the trenches where niceties of behaviour were minimal. Uncle Will felt that four years of trench warfare had coarsened his manners but refrained from criticizing his dandyish host.

We must look briefly at my generation and the two generations which came after mine. Bill (Edward William) my elder brother became a doctor and took over the practice which my easy-going father built up (he of Maynooth fame). Bill's younger son Terry was, in his heyday, Welsh Amateur Golfing Champion and shared the Royal St. David's course record at Harlech. Terry is my nephew: my other nephew Brian is the father of Thomas who is a particle physicist and recently won the Oxford scholarship to CERN in Geneva. My wife Pauline Bewick is a famous artist here in Ireland. Her forebear Thomas Bewick is even more famous. Our daughter Poppy is also a well-known artist. She lives near us in Co. Kerry with her family. Our daughter Holly, likewise a well-known artist, lives with her family in Tuscany.

To avoid what has become increasingly like the grand finale of a nineteenth-century novel, I will call a halt and offer the reins to a new generation.

Appendix IV

Selected artwork by Pat Melia, 1964–2010

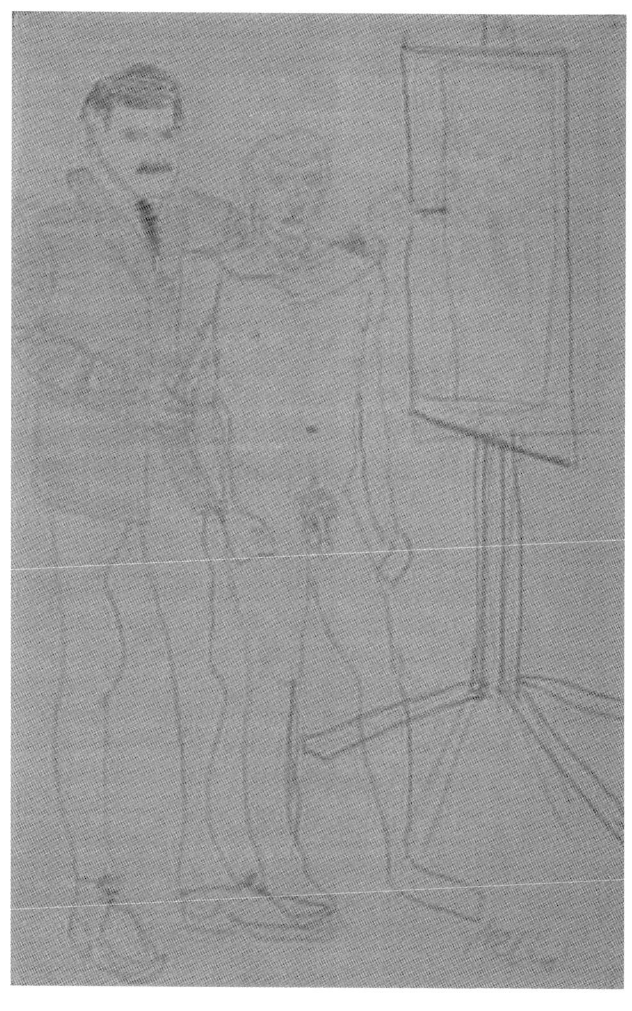

'Pauline Bewick', 1964

Roby Lakatos, Czech Republic violinist, 2004

P.M.

Gortroe, Killarney, 1973

Seán O'Leary in his Puppeteer's Costume
Pat Melia

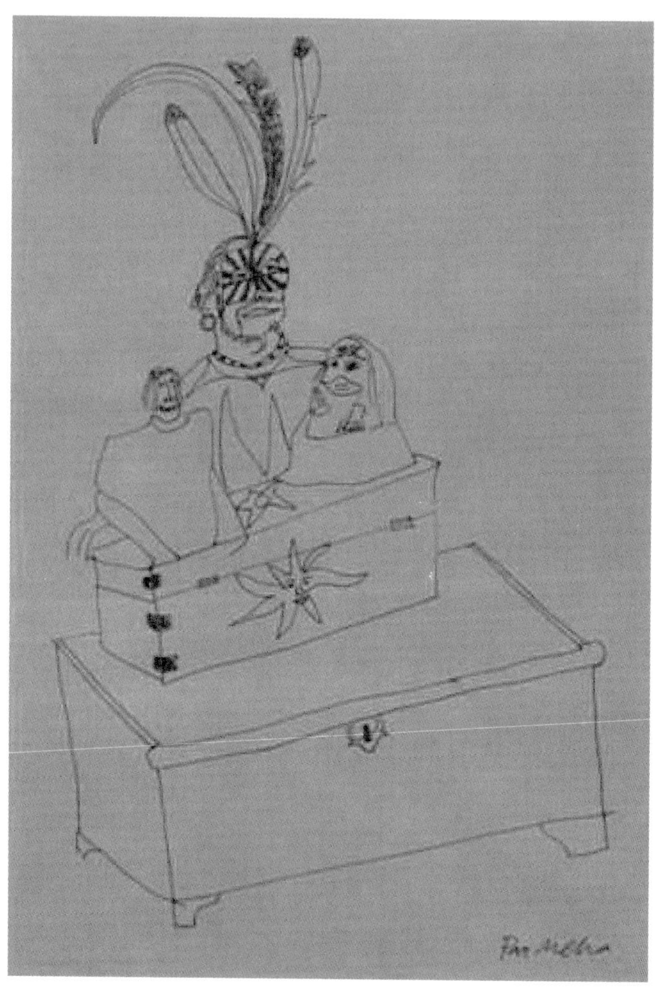

GOL
A.
CA
FE
DE LA MODE

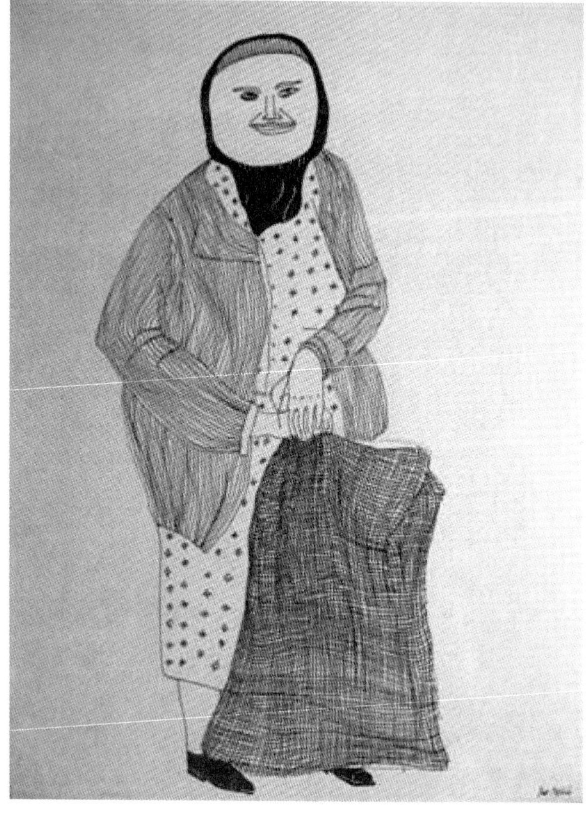

THE TIMES

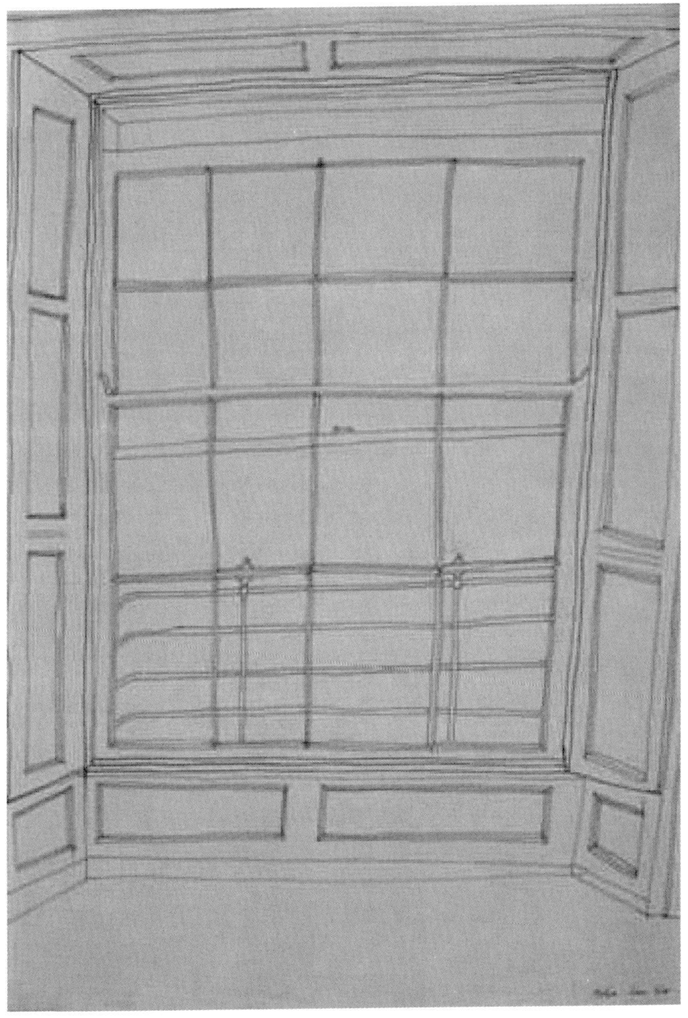

Watercolours, 1996

Watercolour, 1996

pastel, no date

'The Porter Drinkers', oil on board, 24" x 18"

Ciclismo, oil on board, 15" x 11", 1999
Published in the *Chelsea Arts Club 2002 Yearbook*

'Test Match at the Oval', oil on board, 12" x 16", 1998

'The Moorings, Kells Bay', oil on board, 24.5" x 29.5"

'Mr Clement Freud at Naas', oil on board, 14" x 10"

'Mr Clement Freud at Naas'

'Man, Monkey, Mountains, Nepal', oil on board

Gargellan, oil on board

'S. Y. Electra Meets Whale', oil on board, 8" x 10"

'Circus Girl', oil on board

'Castiglione della Pescaia', oil on board

'Puck Fair', oil on board, 76" x 51"

'Trattoria', oil on board

'The Writer at his Breakfast', oil on board, 15" x 11"

RÉPUBLIQUE FRANÇAISE

MINISTÈRE DES TRAVAUX PUBLICS, DES TRANSPORTS ET DU TOURISME

NAVIGATION DE PLAISANCE

PERMIS DE CIRCULATION

M onsieur Philip James CASTLE

de nationalité Britannique

propriétaire du bateau : "CARN INGLI"

est autorisé à effectuer sur les voies navigables, de HAVRE

à LA MEDITERRANEE *, un seul voyage aller et retour,*

du 13 Avril 1960 *au* 31 Décembre *19*60.

Paris, le 12 AVR 1960 *19*

Pour le Ministre et par délégation
P. le Directeur des Ports Maritimes
et des Voies Navigables
L'Administrateur Civil
sous-Directeur de l'Exploitation des
Ports Maritimes et des Voies Navigables

MINISTÈRE DES TRAVAUX PUBLICS & DES TRANSPORTS
P.T.V.N.

T.S.V.P.

I. Le titulaire du présent permis circule avec son bateau à ses risques et périls. Il doit s'assurer auprès des services locaux que son bateau peut passer sans avaries sous les ponts et autres ouvrages d'art, ainsi que dans les écluses.

Il lui est recommandé, en outre, avant de s'engager sur les voies navigables à régime très variable, telles que le Rhône et la Loire, de s'assurer également auprès des services locaux de l'état actuel de navigabilité de ces voies.

II. Le passage aux écluses et ponts mobiles est gratuit.

III. Le présent permis devra être visé par tous les bureaux de contrôle rencontrés, tant au retour qu'à l'aller.

IV. La présente autorisation n'est valable que pour les bateaux de plaisance, à l'exclusion de tous bateaux se livrant à des opérations commerciales.

J. U. 901652. [25978]

VISAS DES BUREAUX DE CONTROLE

TRAJET **ALLER**		TRAJET **RETOUR**	
TIMBRE DES BUREAUX		TIMBRE DES BUREAUX	
BUREAU DE CONTROLE N° 2 ... 31 JUIL 1960 VIVES-EAUX	BUREAU DE CONTROLE N° 14 ... 12 AOUT 1960 ILE-BARBE		
BUREAU DE CONTROLE N° 021 31 JUIL 1960 — CANNES —	BUREAU DE CONTROLE N° 154 13 AOUT 1960 LA MULATIERE		
Bureau de Déclaration de VILLENEUVE-s/-YONNE Enregistré sous le N° ... 2. 8. 60	BUREAU DE CONTROLE N° 188 18 AOUT 1960 PORT-ST-LOUIS		
BUREAU DE CONTROLE L'Agent de ... ECLUSE D'EPINEAU 2 Aout 1960			
BUREAU DE CONTROLE N° 156 le 2. 8. 60 -LAROCHE-			
BUREAU DE CONTROLE N° 24 -5 AOUT 1960 -MONTBARD-			
BUREAU DE CONTROLE N° 024 7/8/60 -POUILLY-			
BUREAU DE CONTROLE N° 129 -9 AOUT 1960 — DIJON —			
Canal de Bourgogne St-JEAN-de-LOSNE - Écluse N° 76 Date 10.8.60 L'Agent			
BUREAU DE CONTROLE N° 224 11 AOUT 1960 VERDUN-SUR-LE-DOUBS			

Le premier bureau de contrôle ne pouvant utiliser ce tableau ajoutera une feuille intercalaire.

SCRAP LOG BOOK

OF THE

CARN INGH

From the Port of SOUTHAMPTON

To AEGEAN

COMMANDED BY

PHILLIP CASTLE

Commencing 19/7/60

Ending ?

KEPT BY

P I MELIA SHIPS DOCTOR + M F LAVERTY FIRST MATE.